Winsome Allure

Illustrated by Sheryll LaFond

Acknowledgement

To my number one fan and support, my husband Brian,
I love you to the moon and back.

Big thanks to my siblings Junnah Rose and Sherwin Jason Silao
for helping me with social media and website.

Shoutout and thanks to my supportive colorist whose colored works
are featured on the back cover of this book;

Cheryl Etheridge
Colleen Diamond
Francoise Gaspari
Margolet van Zyl
Jill Haworth

To my family and friends for their continued prayers and encouragement.

And most of all to God Almighty for His countless blessings.

And to you who purchased this book, I thank you.
I hope coloring each page
will bring you joy and relaxation.

Social Media Information:

facebook.com/ArtbySheryll
instagram.com/sheryll_lafond
twitter.com/SlafondArt
etsy.com/shop/ArtbySheryll

This book belongs to

. . . .

Check out my other coloring books:

Includes 30 single sided pages of my hand-drawn line art
inspired by beautiful, fierce and mystical women and their bond
with nature.

My book Fantabulous Animals Coloring Book is my first published book.
It features illustrations of 35 Animals with patterns.